HOOPS

Also by Major Jackson

Leaving Saturn

HOOPS

poems

Major Jackson

W. W. NORTON & COMPANY   NEW YORK   LONDON

For information about permission to reproduce selections from this book, write to
Permissions, W. W. Norton & Company, Inc.,
500 Fifth Avenue, New York, NY 10110

Manufacturing by Courier Westford
Book design by Anna Oler

Library of Congress Cataloging-in-Publication Data
Jackson, Major, 1968–
Hoops : poems / Major Jackson—1st ed.
p. cm.
ISBN-13 : 978-0-393-05937-3 (hardcover)
ISBN-10 : 0-393-05937-5 (hardcover)
1. Title.
PS3610.A354H66 2006
811'.6—dc22

2005033320

W. W. Norton & Company, Inc., 500 Fifth Avenue, New York, NY 10110
www.wwnorton.com

W. W. Norton & Company Ltd., Castle House, 75/76 Wells Street, London WIT 3QT

2 3 4 5 6 7 8 9 0

for Kristen Johanson

Contents

Selling Out / 13

I

Hoops / 19
Moose / 29
Bum Rush / 32
Silk City / 34
Metaphor / 37
Maddeningly Elusive, Yet Endlessly Tempting / 39

II

Urban Renewal / 43

    XIII. The backyard garden wall is mossy green / 43
    XIV. What he gave of himself lacked the adornment
        of lilacs, / 45
    XV. Back then I had a ceaseless yearning.
        My breathing / 47

XVI. A squeegee blade along your tongue's length. / 48

XVII. What of my fourth-grade teacher at Reynolds
    Elementary, / 49

XVIII. How untouchable the girls arm-locked strutting / 50

XIX. That moment in church when I stared at the reverend's
    black / 51

XX. Out of punctured wounds we spun up, less / 53

III

Letter to Brooks / 57

Fern Rock / 57

Olney / 62

Logan / 68

Wyoming / 73

Hunting Park / 80

Erie / 85

Allegheny / 91

North Philadelphia / 96

Susquehanna-Dauphin / 103

Cecil B. Moore / 108

Girard / 114

Fairmont / 119

Spring Garden / 123

Acknowledgments

Grateful acknowledgment is made to the editors of the following publications in which some of these poems have appeared in earlier drafts:

bornmagazine.com, Callaloo, From the Fishouse, Grand Street, LIT, Rivendell, Third Coast, Triquarterly, Poetry Daily, and *Provincetown Arts.*

"Urban Renewal XVII" appeared in *Pushcart Prize XXIX, Best of the Small Presses* and *Best American Poetry 2004.* I extend appreciation to the editors of those anthologies.

I am also grateful for the sustaining support of The Mrs. Giles Whiting Foundation, The Witter Bynner Foundation, Cave Canem Foundation, Inc., The Fine Arts Work Center, and The Frost Place.

A traditional bow is owed to many friends and colleagues without whose penetrating comments, critical conversations, and lasting encouragement I would have remained enthusiastically in awe yet speechless. They include: Jeffery Renard Allen, Philip Baruth, Emily Bernard, Greg Bottoms, Anthony Bradley, Jilly Dybka, Thomas Sayers Ellis, Nick Flynn, Joanne V. Gabbin,

John Gennari, Huck Gutman, Terrance Hayes, John Hennessy, Laban Carrick Hill, James Hoch, David Huddle, Mat Johnson, Kati and Jim Johanson, Ann Johanson, the *Jazz-Lit.com Arts Collective*, Patricia Spears Jones, Mary Lou Kete, Amor Kohli, Mark LaFlaur, Sebastian Matthews, Gail and Michael Mazur, Todd McGowan, Alison Meyers, Hilary Neroni, Gregory Pardlo, Alan Michael Parker, Ed Pavlić, Robert Polito, Valerie Rohy, Touré, Robyn Warhol, Katharine Whitcomb, Kari Winter, Marion Wrenn, Muriel Wolf, and Jake Adam York.

For her unwavering support and patience, I extend heartfelt thanks to Jill Bialosky.

HOOPS

Selling Out

for Mat Johnson

Off from a double at McDonald's,
no autumnal piñata, no dying
leaves crumbling to bits of colored
paper on the sidewalks only yesterday,
just each breath bursting to explosive fog
in a dead-end alley near Fifth, where on
my knees, with my fingers laced on my head
and a square barrel prodding a temple,
. I thought of me in the afterlife.
Moments ago, Chris Wilder and I
jogged down Girard, lost in the promise
of two girls who winked past pitched
lanes of burgers and square chips
of fish, at us, reigning over grills and vats.
Moments ago, a barrage of beepers
and timers smeared the lengths of our chests.
A swarm of hard-hatted dayworkers
coated in white dust, mothers on relief,
the minimum-waged poor from the fast-
food joints lining Broad, inched us closer
in a check-cashing line towards the window

of our dreams,—all of us anxious to enact
the power of our riches: me in the afterlife.
What did it matter, Chris and I still
in our polyester uniforms caked
with day-old batter, setting out
for an evening of passion marks?
We wore Gazelles, matching sheepskins,
and the ushanka, miles from Leningrad.
Chris said, *Let's cop some blow* despite
my schoolboy jitters. A loose spread
of dealers preserved corners. Then a kid,
large for the chrome Huffy he pedaled,
said he had the white stuff and led us
to an alley fronted by an iron gate on
a gentrified street edging Northern Liberties.
I turned to tell Chris how the night
air dissolved like soil, how jangling
keys made my neck itch, how maybe
this wasn't so good an idea, when
the cold opening of gun-barrel
steel poked my head, and Chris's eyes
widened like two water spills before
he bound away to a future of headphones
and release parties. Me? The afterlife?
Had I ever welcomed back the old
neighborhood? Might a longing
persistent as the seedcorn maggot
tunnel through me? All I know:
a single dog barked his own vapor,
an emptiness echoed through blasted

shells of rowhomes rising above,
and I heard deliverance in the bare
branches fingering a series of powerlines
in silhouette to the moon's hushed
excursion across the battered fields
of our lives, that endless night
of ricocheting fear and shame.
No one survives, no one unclasps
his few strands of gold chains
or hums "Amazing Grace" or pours
all his measly bills and coins into the trembling,
free hand of his brother and survives.
No one is forced facedown and waits
forty minutes to rise and begin again
his march, past the ice-crusted dirt,
without friendship or love, who barely knew
why the cry of the earth set him running,
even from the season's string of lights,
flashing its pathetic shot at cheer—to arrive
here, where the page is blank, an afterlife.

Hoops

for Hank Gathers

I.

By a falling, Cyclone chain-
link fence, a black rush streaks
for netted hoops, & one alone
from a distance breaks

above the undulant pack, soars—
more a Sunday Skywalk,
he cups the ball, whirling his arm,
swoops down a *Tomahawk.*

"Radar! Don't fly without me!"
It's Big Earl who coughs then downs
his bottle, a 40 oz. of Olde E.
Laughter makes its rounds.

I cross a footpath of a city block,
a short rut that snakes between
a lush epitaph of dandelions
& weed-brush behind Happy

Hollow Courts; the ghost
of a staircase echoes here: sign
of lives lived, of souls lost.
Faded hues of graffiti lines

bombed on a wall, *PHASE*
says Don't Stop the Body Rock.
At gate's entrance, my gaze
follows Radar & his half-cocked

jump shot. All morning I sang
hymns yet weighed *his* form:
his flashing the lane, quick-
stop to become sky-born.

Elbows posed like handlebars,
he flicks a wrist, the pill arcs
through sunlight glare,
& splashes the basket's

circle of air. A Boom Box bobs
& breaks beats on a buckling sea
of asphalt;—the hard,
driving rhymes of BDP,

rousing that rowdy crowd
of hustlers tossing craps, waging
fists & dollar bets, only louder—
& one more enraged

promises to pistol-whip
the punk who doesn't pay.
He doubles up, blows a kiss;
each dealer counts his days.

I turn from these highlights—
Spaldings missile like meteors.
Radar dribbles near. "You're late."
Before I speak a word,

"My boy, shootin' geometry!"
We laugh. Father Dave, coach
at St. Charles, once let me
play as a walk-on in hopes

I would tutor Radar. Not even
Pythagoras could awaken
in his head the elegance
of a triangle's circumference.

Four years later, he's off
on scholarship to UNC.
I'm to study Nabokov
at state's university.

Proof of Pop-pop's maxim,
"There's more ways to skin . . ."
If the slum's our dungeon,
school's our Bethlehem.

Yet what connects those dots
that rattle hustlers's palms
with Radar's stutter step
& my pen's panopticon?

It casts shadows dark
as tar as we begin
our full-court run. A brick
off the half-moon's side

—in waves, we sprint.
No set offence: his pass,
my bounce, his deft
lateral, two-hand jam.

II.

Stark Sunday afternoon light,
unending solo of sky,
a parade of leaps
& weaves fortifying

our store of groans, each
glistening muscle surging towards
the body's curative peaks,—
nimble, sprung, absorbed

in our picks, touch, & rolls,
we swerve across haloed

turf whose ceremony overruns
suffering, an arpeggio

of chucks, split-second lobs
past a squad of sweat-backed
ghosts,—pass, glide,
post, pivot away, look

then dish: follow through,—
Swish! Radar backpedals
as the net strings flap & swing to
rest. The blacktop ripples,

raising its curtain of steam;
five ballers grudgingly exit
& make for the next team.
Top of the key, hand on hip,

I point for art sake, for jest
a finger,—challenge
Radar in a dunking contest.
Just then a car engine

revs Oxford Ave., stalls & peels
out: panther-like Camaro
whose chrome wheels
screech to a stop. Its smoke-

tinted window drops diplomatic-
ally; a frenzied rustling

rising like shrieks fumbling
inside a scream, & the rusted

base of pole where life
snakes an open cut
up to center court, there lay
Radar enfolding his heart.

III.

The ceiling in my room
a projector's canvas, the moon
a flurried cone of light
to which I recite Brooks,

Frost, Hughes. Lying back
in my mind, each book's
a slide held up like a snap
-shot, giant stills illumined

by that Cyclops's eye.
Below bunk my cousin
stacks tens, twenties,—
pacing corners till twelve,

he & the Ooh-mob Gang
slinging plastic vials
of crack, the cursed slang
of death: "I'm gonna buy

a Gucci watch, Air Nikes,
the hypest gear to look Fly."
dazed he says then cocks
a Wesson; what spells

in the ovals of dead
men's eyes? Other circles
festoon above my head,
O's on the tongue

& bitter to the edge:
"We / Die soon."
A darkness spreads—
at first as clouds float

-ing like this craft's spirited
march, then arise
faces of friends resting
in caskets: Deshaun,

Darnell, Lil Mike,
Shantel, a slide show
whose carousel double-quick
click ricochets shots

across this elegiac. Gazing
its portraits I muse, "This
ceiling's more their grave."
then lower my eyes to toss

my grief on the shelf of their
sinking coffin, beside
that lone rose laid for dear
parting & hear rise from earth

the hurt motto bred
(as my pen's pitch of dirt
pyramids my dread):
"Fuck tomorrow; that's

how I'm living kid. Fuck
tomorrow." It was Tupac
on the waves: *Thugged
to Life*. By song's end,

he's martyred again.
My cousin lounges back
inside the rap's refrain,
fingering his square sack

of spliff. He lip-syncs
his resurrected lyrics.
His pain shrinks
to drags of dialect.

IV.

A morning truck grates
by grinding waste;

a bus at the corner hisses,
and so Radar life erases.

Overnight a muralist
bombed a portrait,
your *Daily News* All-City
dunk. Inside the pill: *R.I.P.*

& the too few years hemmed
between the cupped hands
of parentheses. Children mosey
like indifferent supermen

passing the liquor storefront.
The leastwise drunks
line up as if for a wage,—
the state unrolling its cage.

With no where to go,
a cortege of suped-up low
riders blares up the street.
A rapt motorcade beats

the crew cool inside alone,
head-nodding their own
extinction. All's blasé.
What use the phrase *Tolle*

et lege or the graffiti artist's
heroic tags? A sneaker's a cave.
The legions of lines my fist
inscribes calls back your days.

Moose

After free throws,
He *Swished*, swore up,
& down he could snuff
The ball, both eyes closed.

His right arm stretched farther
Than his hooked left—
Slow-moving, ominous,
Bull-dozer stiff.

Jump shots fired off
Sideways like a windshield
Wiper; its arc ended spinning
Through a ring of steel.

He thought himself a Tarheel,
His jersey, skin-like—
He bounced the pill down
Hard the way one strikes

A spike. If the ball sank,
If the net strings snapped
Then coiled, *Butter Baby*.
No telling his handicap.

But we drove the lane—
Soared on our tippy
Toes, entered a rhythm
Of Pick & Roll,

Give & Go & he'd
Run to his favorite spot,
Off alone, out, our
Orbiting afronaut.

Fed up, he charged
Headfirst, grunt,
Flung his bulk of a body
& rushed nonstop.

Chumps ran, let him
Paw the rock with short
Precise strokes till
He struck & stole

The pill, lumbering
Down court, hunchbacked,
The ball cupped for
His gawky layup.

He fouled like an ogre
From another world
& we laughed, frightened
At how he mirrored

The body on defense,
Playing up close, ghoulish,
Lacking grace, afraid
He'd go face-to-face.

Bum Rush

Dinner at Time Café, I am reminded
   of Shirley Jackson's "The Lottery,"
how a small town piled stones,
   the size of cannonballs and pelted

a mother, like yours or mine, wearing
   her faded housedress and favorite pair
of slippers when she had drawn the black,
   spotted paper from a splintered black box.

How it happens: her flailing arms
   and hands suddenly dropped,
pips of granite nuts, smooth
   and jagged, rough and level,

knocking her cheekbones, clumps
   of blood mingling with dust
when she fell in the garden of stones.
   What will prevent these seventy,

eighty or so epicureans warmed
   by dinner talk and the scent of lamb
from lifting my heart with a fork's light
   flick? To what mountain do I pray

when this mob gathers round
    to offer my loins to a sky hungry
for sacrifice? It's the feeling I get
    watching the numbers fall

in a crowded elevator or when the El
    plunges just before my stop into
an unspeakable darkness. And yet,
    I think it started with the dream,

coming up short, the gang descending
    upon me like a fog of vultures.
When I turn, a flurry of fists,
    the sky, a collage of light. The night

I saw my mother last, I mumbled
    through the evening, kicking
and biting back at the inevitable,
    a world of strangers. In cafés,

I stare at heaps of potatoes, fearful
    of reliving that walk in the snow
away from her grave towards
    a herd of men and children.

Silk City

No space
at the bar
so you stare
at the neon

signs blinking
in the mirror
behind the bottles.
Tiny flecks

of a stuccoed
ceiling glitter.
At a cocktail
table, colors flare

from a lava lamp,
illuminating
a couple bent
towards each other

like angels stilled
in a kiss. The disco
ball whirls, spinning
slow beams of light

from a million
lighthouses. You've
paid to enter so much
darkness. A shore

of human flesh
mingles. A crew
of cool cats lean
against glass

bricked windows,
bobbing heads,
peeping women
in strappy dresses

& ass-huggin' bell
bottoms. The rhythm
hits you like a slow
punch. There's the DJ,

hunched over turn-
tables, leaving
his crates & crates
of vinyl; one hand

holding his head,
nodding in agreement
to the beats'
unbroken enthymatic

claims, the other
spinning moods
& vibes so intoxicating
you throw back

your gin & tonic
& head for the
dance floor. It's time
to lose yourself.

The whole city is
here swiveling on
a throb. You bounce
back & forth in

front of speakers
stacked like blocks to
heaven. The dance floor's
a warm sky when

a woman joins your cipher.
Her eyes roll black,
vinyl-like. Inside you, so
many thresholds to find.

Metaphor

Me and my cousin
would pretend watchtower
on the third floor

of my grandfather's
house Saturdays after
a rainstorm and wait

for white flashes hushed
in a charcoal sky. Crowded
with rooftops, the tiniest

twinkle sent our fingers
off jabbing the air—
Hot icicles! Flying juice!

Zig-zag bolts! Actually,
seen at the margins
of vision, they were less

jagged, oval-shaped
much like electric eels,
smoother around the edges.

For hours, we pointed
then named the sparks,
depending on a rumble

to announce their coming,
auguring like ancient
prophets. My cousin once

compared the many silvery flares
to God's wounds healed
upon human sight. I followed

likening the meteoric openings
to glowing keyholes into
an alien world. Years later,

I would caress a woman
and discover again jewelry
shimmering in the dark.

Maddeningly Elusive, Yet Endlessly Tempting

Like a far-off scream, like a mannequin leaning back-seat
into other mannequins careening, it could stand
for something. Just about. But gauzy and gray,
great slabs ease over, and root-like stems wither.
The radio plays, reducing us to a point; laugh and laugh,
even as a box of Kleenex scraps your hand.
The neighborhood sparks and becomes that blue haze,—
screams inside of screens, which will not stop the coming
of frost, only more frames. If I said, "All ants are fascist,"
would that be the comic turn? When the eyes fill up
(a kind of composting?), an occasion dresses for the
    mountainside:
Mardi Gras in the hills, downpour of skeins,
each brilliant, spiraling suicide a paper float like this one, here.
But then a father sets his pieces on a chessboard
the way a painter spreads out vials of colors
on a windowsill, and even this reminds me of emptying
brown bags of groceries: always first, cauliflower,
the little white trees felled in the bins, then miniature
vats of yogurt, then slender bodies of asparagus
dry-heaving beneath blankets of plastic. A woman sets
her keys on the counter through involuntary sniggers.
Something releases, like a red balloon one forgets

one never owned, and in her right eye she feels
emancipation, and in her left the swell of peppermint
pulls her towards the center of a far-off cry.
Then something else lets go, the ancient wetness
of clouds washing the sidewalks of memory.
Here and there, smoke rises from asphalt
like tranquil fires smouldering or fog lifting
like so many dead at once, that eternal chorus hurts.

Urban Renewal

XIII.

The backyard garden wall is mossy green
and flakes a craggy mound of chips. Nearby
my grandfather kneels between a row of beans
and stabs his shears into earth. I squint an eye,—
a comma grows at his feet. The stucco's
an atlas, meshed-wire continents with leaders
who augured hate, hence ruins, which further sow
discontent. We are weeding, marking borders,
a million taproots stacked in shock. Forty years
from a three-story, he has watched the neighborhood,—
postwar marble steps, a scrubbed frontier
of Pontiacs lining the curb, fade to a hood.
Pasture of wind-driven litter swirls among greasy
bags of takeouts. Panicles of nightblasts
cap the air, a corner lot of broken TVs empties
and spills from a suitcase of hurt. Life amassed,
meaningless as a trampled box of Cornflakes.
When a beggar cupped for change outside
a check-cashing place then snatched his wallet,
he cleaned a .22 revolver & launched this plot. Tidal
layers of cement harden men born gentle as the root

crops tended south, the city its own bitter shrine.
We crouch by watering cans. He pulls a paradise of kale
and shakes root-dirt that snaps like a shadow lost in time.
Tomato vines coil by a plot of herbs. Far from the maddening
caravan of fistfights, jacked-rides, drunkards,
my pen takes aim from the thumbnail of his yard.

XIV.

What he gave of himself lacked the adornment of lilacs,
purple-dotting a ribbon of darkened-shrubs along the floodplain
of the Schuylkill. Notational, for sure, but that's
what open-palms when he flips pocket-like a past, grains
and smatterings of a nifty life foregone, like the world cruise
before the rain of blue jeans. Down-shifting East River Drive's
winding stream of sweeps and hooks, my grandfather and I
   perused
once after a sudden dip, in the stretch it takes to recognize
something significant as one's breathing, a bronzed John B.
Kelly rowing without end, the memorial sculpture of his former
boss, who won Olympic medals but could not scull the Henley
Royal Regatta, as not to sully the Thames with Irish bricklayers.
Jack Sr.'s ballots for mayor pitched and swelled
the bottom of the Delaware. No amount of Monacan
crowns or Hitchcock thrillers could propel the Kellys
up the Main Line. What W.A.S.P. would sign? *No Hibernians
Need Pay* or 6° to Princess Grace. In high school,
I imagined posing in a Sperry Topsider ad, a member
of the sailing team, lined up with oars for flags, our leisured cool
and frat-boy smiles, the dark side of Boathouse Row. Her

closest entry in the Social Registry found her playing Hope
Montgomery Scott, known heiress for whom *The Philadelphia
Story*
told of pedigree. The Kellys groped for power,
and we, affiliation. My grandfather points at the skyline's glory
he once scaffolded, "We gave the city light with those towers."

XV.

Back then I had a ceaseless yearning. My breathing
was older than me, and I moved to the body's core beat,
each step towards the neighborhood garden, a satisfying lecture
on how fingers fall silent in wallets. I learned to speak
under a straw hat and banked it rich on the other side
of a vestibule. I valued only forecasts culled on yellow pads.
Dreams of endless toil stained my cronies, their lips
caked with gossip. In a lounger by a window, I chat
about the Phillies. Bolt locks grow rapidly all around.
If I hustle to the finish, it's only a benign grunt. If I leave
a milk bottle outside, it's because I'm romantic and like
my doorbells ringing. Either way, I know a listening glass
slides along the other side of a wall. It's only homework.
Impressed flowers stretch along my cheek when I sleep.
Aging and gray, my leisure is a hand-me-down, two-bit notice.
A black rotary phone rests on a side table dark as a pistol.
Row-home plaster is transparent, more façade.
With my feet propped, I ponder the sheer surface of longing,
the raucous music of flesh impervious to dishonor.

XVI.

A squeegee blade along your tongue's length.
Most dances are crimes against the face. Ash is
a mirror, & mornings you'll wake not particularly heroic,
but eager to glisten like the silvering of office panes,
light gilding down between your teeth. Make easy listening.
Sigh & gargle. Freedom? Fierce attention to dirt
one might possess. Remember Sonny Boy Sam,
back-door windows & Flava Flav. Subdue a grin, yet mouth—
Well-mannered, soft, an entrance, a conference room.
Oh! Rossi? That's Italian. But the lady said he was
Puerto Rican. All the stoops and dreams, trileveled
seats of speculation, which foam like portraits of deeds
mist, blur, first as vaporish powder, blue crystals
ground-fine, then spume, rain-bowed bubblings.
Now, you are classical, at least your eyes, marble-white,
tinge and tingle: fresh, newly heard harmonies.

XVII.

What of my fourth-grade teacher at Reynolds Elementary,
who weary after failed attempts to set to memory
names strange and meaningless as grains of dirt around
the mouthless, mountain caves at Bahrain Karai:
Tarik, Shanequa, Amari, Aisha, nicknamed the entire class
after French painters whether boy or girl. Behold
the beginning of sentient formless life. And so,
my best friend Darnell became Marcel, and Tee-tee
was Braque, and Stacy James was Fragonard,
and I, Eduard Charlemont. The time has come to look
at these signs from other points of view. Days passed
in inactivity before I corrected her, for Eduard was
Austrian and painted the black chief in a palace in 1878
to the question whether intelligence exists. All of Europe
swooned to Venus of Willendorf. Outside her tongue,
yet of it, in textbooks Herodotus tells us of the legend
of Sewosret, Egyptian, colonizer of Greece,
founder of Athens. What's in a name? Sagas rise and
fall in the orbs of jump ropes, Hannibal grasps a Roman
monkey bar on history's rung, and the mighty heroes at recess
lay dead in woe on the imagined battlefields of Halo.

XVIII.

How untouchable the girls arm-locked strutting
up the main hall of Central High unopposed
for decades looked. I flattened myself against
the wall, unnerved by their cloudsea of élan,
which pounced upon any timid girl regrettably
in their way, their high-wattage lifting slow motion
like curls of light strands of honey. The swagger
behind their blue-tinted sunglasses and low-rider
jeans hurt boys like me, so vast the worlds
between us, even the slightest whiff of recognition,
an accidental side glance, an unintended tongue-piercing
display of Juicy Fruit chew, was intoxicating
and could wildly cast a chess-playing geek into
a week-long surmise of inner doubts, likelihoods,
and depressions. You might say my whole life led
to celebrating youth and how it snubs and rebuffs.
Back then I learned to avoid what I feared
and to place my third-string hopes on a game-winning
basketball shot, sure it would slow them to a stop,
pan their lip-glossed smiles, blessing me with their cool.

XIX.

That moment in church when I stared at the reverend's black
kente-paneled robe & sash, his right hand clasping the back
of my neck, the other seizing my forehead, standing
in his *Watch this* pose, a leg behind him ready to spring,
his whole body leaning into the salvation of my wizened soul,
I thought of the Saturday morning wrestlers of my youth who'd
    hold
their opponents till they collapsed on a canvas in a slumberous
heap, and how it looked more like a favor, a deed, though
    barbarous,
a graceful tour out of this world, that chthonic departure
back to first waters, and wondered what pains I endured
in Mr. Feltyburger's physic's class, worshipping light, density,
    mass,
preferring to stare long at snowdomes or the carcasses
of flies pooling above in the great fluorescent cover, and how beds
are graves, my mother and father kissing each other's head,
their cupped faces unhurriedly laying the other down,
and how all locked embraces light in my mind from below
in blue-neon like you'd find on the undercarriage of sports cars,
and then what came was the baker stacking her loaves,

one by one, into little coffers, and Desdemona's
last surrender to Othello's piercing glance, and Isaac shown
a militia of clouds over Moriah, and the dying we submerge
in a baptism of pillows, and how we always loiter at this verge,
there, between rising up and falling back, as in now, this tank
of sound I swim in, gripped between the push and yank
of his clutch, caught in that rush of tambourines next to solemn
trays of grape juice and bits of crackers held by deacons when
the reverend, serious as a pew, whispered, "Fall back, my son.
    Fall."

XX.

Out of punctured wounds we spun up, less
the phoenix, dive-bombers still. I am haunted
by shapes of trees, one whose arms, an excess
of mounts, from which ever leapers we vaulted,—
passing, flash-like semblances of flight.
This is where Darren measured absence round
visible stars the night his dad punched the bright
smile of his mother into a soundless
hole, where Wilbur went on a famine strike
scaling ten branches a day to purity,
to grace. Because her sister touched and stroked
her till she was gleaming and sticky,
Sam climbed so high we lost her shadow,
obscured by overstory's thickening
lines. Scalloped leaves trickled below,
brittle telegrams. I sought the quickening
gaze of the dusky flycatcher and listened
to the greenish-black like a secret pitched
between a pair of crickets. No hungers, no wind
swayed the top of our corner's paperback mapleleaf,

for Jamie. A nameless hurt so deep, he leapt
the farthest, a branchless fall to his death,
from the top of Blumberg Housing Projects.

III

Letter to Brooks

FERN ROCK

1.

Dear Gwendolyn—or is it Dear Madam?
   Or as Quraysh would more likely say
Mama Gwen. He, unlike orphaned Adam,
   Had you no less arriving to the fray,
   That surrogate mentor-friend who pays
Art's admission fee. Only since your absence
Our tour's been self-guided. Anthologists

2.

Disagree, respectfully of course—for what
   Is a corpus but the Spirit on foot?
On such ground I begin my epistolary chat,
   Although I gather you'd prefer we strut
   On through, fisted pens raised imaging truth.
Plus up there you must I bet have other
Celestial errands with which to bother.

3.

I consulted Langston my son on this point
  Who thought you now in charge of lyres
& harps, tuning strings, adorning joints—
  An answer he imagined I'd like to hear,
  The professorial poet whose overbear
-Ing view, children best fulfill dad's dreams,
Thus prove black laureates lurk in the genes.

4.

How vain, too, parents who schedule
  A child's every waking hour: from ballet
Instruction to sailing camps to, as usual,
  A learning of the scales. Horseplay's
  For the under-classed lazy. I've heard say
Mattel is to market kiddy PalmPilots,—
Or was it (oh, shoot!) laptops for tots?

5.

I write from Colorado at my desk
  In the Magnolia Hotel. This week's
Poet-in-residence, I feel Audenesque,
  Having traveled this far to mount & speak
  On the habits of my muse or to critique
Student poems, staying mostly honest,
Till a line, like this, begets cardiac arrest.

6.

I should have donned an oxygen mask;
    Breathing here comes in fits and starts. Last
Night, reciting poems, between words, short intakes
    Of breath which made their stress lusty,
    Urgent, a collage of gasps as if life
Were panting out like a morning glory
In the end, tight-lipped, a memento mori.

7.

My hosts are cheerful, delighted I've come
    The distance. They stomach my eccentric
Air, regard me a linguistical phenom.
    Who sports floppy hats and eats carrot sticks,
    Speak in non sequiturs more to affix
The idea they're getting their money's worth:
Platonic poet heads above planet Earth.

8.

I'll dash this note off promptly; I've checked
    My itinerary. I'm off on a visit
To North Denver High and to be picked
    Up any minute. The unseen benefits
    Of words I'll promote. On cannabis
I'll be most emphatic, "Kids, deign to avoid.
You'll likely catch the paranoids."

9.

I take my cue, as you have likely guessed,
    From the recent bloom of epistles.
Doty's "Letter to Walt Whitman," his largesse
    Of fraternal pluck, make many an apostle.
    But several reads after, the muscle
Of Auden's eye had me finally concede
One's growth relies on one's gift to exceed

10.

One's reach. So, I hope this note is welcomed,
    Your kindnesses being legendary,
Death failing to place a moratorium
    On poets' fan mail, yours especially.
    Michael S. Harper et al. brazenly
Claim your work eminent among the boys,
Your pen's the equal of Chaucer, Dante, Joyce.

11.

Reprints assure postal bins stay full.
    You're not likely to receive death threats.
Be wary wax-sealed envelopes bearing skulls.
    A deaf critic is a cause for fret,—
    Albeit doubtful packages of anthrax
Should arrive at heaven's pearly gates,
Doubtful, too, Hugh Hefner & his playmates.

12.

I contemplated sending by e-mail.
   We've gone gaga over the Inbox.
Each in his cell blinking forward fulfills
   Globalism's promise: round-the-clock
   Friendships; a forum for every boycott.
Electronic petitions are a bit of a drag.
How many times will the NEA be bagged?

13.

Thousands of fingers, even now as I write,
   Draw near the keyboard's ENTER key
In hopes of keeping at bay the strange sight
   Of their faces reflected in the screen
   Or the dreadful lie that life is but a dream:
The mean world seen through the inflated tear
Callous enough to ignore our reckless fears.

OLNEY

1.

Why write to you? I cannot envision
    A more enigmatic woman who demands
Greater attention, so many questions
    Linger. I thought of you in Ireland
    While biking the countryside, my hand
Swept aside a delicate mist of longing,
And I saw myself with my childhood gang

2.

On the stoop where we played Hearts for dimes,
    Slap-boxed, or simply posed against a ride,
Crotch-cupping. Those lush green Irish plains
    Fell on the upclimb, yet the expanse was wide,
    So I suffered the exile's self-afflicting, evil-eyed
Probe. I would have felt as alien in Sierra Leone.
What was I doing so far from home?

3.

I recalled at once your well-spun phrase:
   "Puzzled wreckage / Of the middle passage."
Bewilderment bores, true—still, amazing:
   Your lines give weight to baggage.
   Art's doing is to lift the sheet off the cage;
The psychic wounds within rendered bite-sized,
Pertinent, grave: our selves no longer disguised.

4.

The next pub I chose I raised a dark pint,
   Then another: to you and my acute
Isolation, to the hoodwinked, the *Niña*, the *Pinta*,
   & Sinterklaas, to my urban canticle,
   To Yeats, to rugby, to British cutlasses,
To clean-shaven heads and black Doc Martens,
To stampeding hoofs rounding the margins,

5.

To flags of fear I raised in Skibbereen,
   To nationalists in Belfast, Donegal, and Dublin,
To tweeded tourists, to middle-class imaginings
   Of coats of arms where heraldry gilds the skin:
   Bobo out of paradise wears Ralph Lauren,
To bagpipes soothing the American caste,
To class ascension and dignified pasts;

6.

To Ireland and its convincing show
    Of ale and class, & self-conceptions
That bruise, to our vulnerable muse, kow-
      Towing to the times. Let's take exception
      To decrees where aesthetics né precepts
Based on continents, eye colors, or looks
Produce poems whose centers go uncooked.

7.

The bar empty I surveyed the length
    Of my bottle, outside the pastoral view.
What I longed for? The medicinal imprint
      Of skyscrapers, the proverbial tennis shoe,
      A power line, or night pavements which knew
My mind's folds. But, no Carl Orff given
To drinking songs, I learned to enliven

8.

The *Luftmensch* in me. Mornings I visit
    The sports page to learn last night's score.
My car radio's tuned to Top 40. I commit
      To memory Oscar nominees, for
      The age underlooks its importance,—nor
The Sunday crossword would I likely complete
If I could not name the king of popular beats.

9.

Fukuyama got it right: we've reached
    The end of poetry (smart reader: allow
In earnest this fallacy). The last man's deep
    -Seated longings having evolved, now
    Prefab his urges and feelings which bow
To set stimuli hurtful as fast-food close-ups:
Styrofoam hash browns, billboard coffee cups.

10.

Yet, explain it thus: remembrance of life
    Summoned in a stroke or song or delivered
In a few lines of verse should somehow lift,
    Steady us more: the meandering river,
    The embraced body held as it shivers,
A waning sky, a fiery scream at dusk,
Baked blueberries spilling from a pie crust.

11.

No doubt you'll pardon these digressions,
    Enjoying a life absent of hours to read.
Detours add to a sightseer's possessions.
    We're all the richer when artists feed
    The mind's thirst with things to see than proceed
Like a train between points A & B, never out
To explore as many views to talk about.

12.

Although the Rockies do not picture
    Firm in my window, I'm aware they're there—
White peaks cresting gives texture
    To rose-light dusting the sky. I stared
    On my way here and turned my cab fare
To a docent's fee, having asked the long
Ride in. A sutured horizon stretched along,

13.

& my guide, a man hacking through phlegm,
    Gestured with his head, "That's Columbine."
& hacked again, his soundtrack to the cam
    Capturing bodies slayed by bombs & Tec-9s
    As if the allegory of living were the crime.
We must not speak it: we're doomed to playact
Our outlaw past. Our psychopathic,

14.

Trenchcoat children whisper in civics class
    The 2nd Amendment like the fate
Of a prayer, then open fire en masse—
    In combat protecting the state
    From aliens? On a murderous march of hate,
Our genetically enhanced super-soldiers
Leave bodies for dead: Martians, human, deer.

15.

The light's blinking red on the telephone,
    Which means I've likely missed my summons.
My escort awaits. I'll have to postpone,
    Pack my shoulder bag, make it on the run.
    Before I jet though let me list off, one
By one, potential postmarks from various states—
Oh, I should just go. I'm dreadfully late.

LOGAN

1.

A halyard peals and resounds this clear morning
    Over Torch Lake. Its empty clang
Accents the joy I feel by contrast. *Dithering*
    Heights is what we've come to name
    The in-laws's summer, Bellaire home. The aim
Here, to rest as hard as you can, or race in as
Many of the club's sailing regattas.

2.

I stay dockside, but on occasion will crew.
    Being as I have as much experience
As flying a plane, there's not much for me to do,
    Except duck when we tack lest I'm knocked past
    Tense. I prefer to watch from a distance
With a chilled glass of white. My feet propped up
As Big Jim maneuvers to win the cup.

3.

The beauty of the angled sails pacing
    On the horizon I liken to
A covey of Brancusi's *Bird[s] in Space*,
    Thus supporting Levi-Strauss's view
    The signified and signifier breaking in two,
Abstraction speeds up the divorce;
O, the pleasures of a conceptual horse.

4.

You were the Empress of the Portrait. Take
    "The Sundays of Satin-Legs Smith." Abiding,
Pimped-out now princely in gold, he pulsates
    In splashes of music videos, a glittering
    Sham, wrists thrust out diamond bling
His need, sparked by an inner charge to adorn—
Visibility he seeks, thus a man to scorn.

5.

The black intellect is no different, is she?
    Baldwin's fierce saunter up rue de Verneuil
Petal collar blazed up flashed fain Paris,—
    Too shadowy here, Saint Germain's vernal
    Blossoming of café dwellers became art's infernal
Jamboree of brains where Wright and Himes
Stylized, too, their sidewalk stares, making them

6.

Super-luminal, the modernist trick
    Of burnishing—self-exile, the gold tooth
In the cerebral's mouth. Pound flipped
    In a Venetian recording booth;
    Wystan traded faded Albion for youthful
Guys on 52nd; a Parisian atelier
Christened Radnitsky Man Ray.

7.

Rare is the change of Leroi in Cuba
    To *Black Magic* Imamu to Amiri,
Vitriolic critic of the petit bourgeois,
    Who caught Fidel's fire, who, wary
    Of commissions, backs the conspiracy
Theory that the Twin Towers fated
Fall was powerfully orchestrated.

8.

Like John Kennedy's assassination,
    Will we ever know? The tragedies
That widely befall such a nation
    As ours, someone's likely to keep the keys
    To glitches and muffs. The strategies
Of damage control and spin beat out truth.
Democracies earn their sleuths.

9.

Here's one of those rhetorical questions
    I'm likely to abuse. Poetry is full of them—
The rule being no poet has solutions,
    At least ones who make nothing happen:
    "What gave?" ask the critics. The conversion
In '67 at Fisk? Why dull the edge
Of a weapon? Why hand over your badge?

10.

Yusef muses: you suffered in your skin,
    As if *Maud Martha* were a portal
Through the blue-black cold to "Being Gwen-
    Dolyn Brooks." And we, your dark kin, mortals
    Montaged till our hate's a single portrayal:
You carried aloft on the oeuvre of your hearse—
We line the curbs and weep on our hurts.

11.

More distressing than imperial war,
    These lines will land on clogged ears,
Will ne'er jump-start modern delight for
    Reading habits like Top 40 I fear
    Make what's fashionable soon dreary,
E.g., L=A=N=G=U=A=G=E poetry; the darling
Of the runway once, now lacks a farthing's

12.

Worth of mystique: her legs aged, her eyes
    Tapped of all glitz and indifference.
She's the tragic, flash-in-the-pan vamp eyeing
    A café window. Epicureans
    Dining on decadence, eerily Darwinian.
What age granted these lines material good?
Can the epistolary form contain our hoods?

WYOMING

1.

Your own Social Aid & Pleasure
  Club, your benevolence seemed old world,
So many checks bestowed; your signature
  Was scripture spreading the good word:
  "Where there is no gift there is no art," the pearl
Even Wm. Gates finds spiritually enhancing,
Proof every Medici knows, "Giving is good living."

2.

Which reminds me,—no adequate Thank You
  Conveys the perennial debt I owe,
That morning you chose to forgo the choo-
  Choo to Manhattan. Instead, my stereo
  VW played Kravitz's "Flowers for Zoë"
On cruise control as we schlepped up I-95—
The weight of your fate in part kept us alive.

3.

Although too many showings can be a chore,
    You stopped in Philly at the Painted Bride,
Your esteemed Jefferson Lecture tour.
    True to reputation, you inscribed
    Copies of books for the many meek-eyed
Admirers, giving each your full presence.
At twelve, I thought, "Brooks for President."

4.

Everyone knows you rarely took off
    In a flying machine, the railway
Your preferred choice of travel. A chauf
    -Feur, still, is best when one wants by day
    Affable company to chat away
The prior night's tensile stress or to court
A fresh disciple disguised as one's escort.

5.

Jersey, the industrial carcass, one
    Of the great literary states we agreed
Which, of course, begged the question
    About landscape: Does a poet's muse need
    Her own wasteland to succeed?
Then, to each a refinery or a smokestack
Or junkie in the alley with a baseball bat.

6.

I felt less the stranger, something in you
    That carried at once the high dignity
Of your calling (seldom practiced by few)
    As the face of a race, and the sprightly
    Girl still in awe. The world freaks with Foxy.
We've lost the uplift, the decorum and light.
Can you picture Li'l Kim in a Rohan Crite?

7.

I struck up conversation about "Riot"
    Somewhere near Newark International;
John Cabot, condescension not-
    Withstanding, seemed a sacrificial
    Figure, martyr on the altar of racial
Warfare, his plunge beneath the will of the folk
No less woeful hidden by blood & smoke.

8.

To which you replied, "Absolutely not."
    (Seems I pushed the limits of your munificence.)
For you, Cabot was more than a bigot;
    His brand of intolerance? Transcendent,
    Given wings by a rank aestheticism, hence
You could not afford an ounce of empathy
For snobs who rose above humanity.

9.

Still feeling the sting of your rebuttal,
    (More the misread artist's reprimand)
We pulled over. Nice! The Plaza Hotel,
    Central Park South. A black-caped doorman
    Jaunted curbside, opened your door, "Welcome
Back Ms. Brooks." His words allayed fears
You'd be hurt while in my care,

10.

An anxiety brought on by a wide-eyed
    Worship, mark of the afflicted
Would-be author longing to join the tide
    Of shadows thinking. The conflicted
    Liaison H. Bloom sought to depict
Seems flawed; ephebes love their precursors—
It's their words that are the worst oppressors.

11.

The venetians failed to close. We gave
    Ceilings their only glances and gasped
Like pages at light opening. "How brave,"
    We said, "petals inside bubbles." Grass
    Spread up a door. Auteurs donned masks
Then swapped their names for eternal time.
Books stacked up,—the spine of mankind.

12.

What fevered my wrist was this: you could
    Have amicably thanked me for the ride,
Extending your elbow-length glove, you could
    Have disappeared in that opulent façade,
    Instead you asked if I'd read alongside
That night. I left and bought a pad from Kmart
Then wrote all the poems I knew by heart,

13.

Which numbered two,—one of those, a haiku.
    The evening thickens dense as trees
Except the feel of reading on stage with you.
    Truth be told, I've come to believe such deeds
    Define as much the black tradition and seed
The garden Clarence Major speaks. If it thrives,
Scores bend on hand and knee keeping it alive.

14.

As much I deem firm black poets cultivate
    A knack at verse, without sponsors
Beating drums manuscripts disintegrate.
    Think Wheatley growing silent in a drawer
    Or the world having never read Harper's
Dear John, Dear Coltrane, one you saw to light—
Think Dr. King tom-tomming civil rights.

15.

Ted Joans sat in the audience, hip
    I recall, back from "who-knows-where," a sharp,
Red, bow tie altered a beard which flourished
    Full round his avuncular face. He remarked
    On your role as poetry's matriarch.
Then tossed from a pocket a flower,
"La plus belle Africaine in your honor."

16.

I love that photo I dug up online,
    He and Ginsberg puckering for a smooch,
The way a snapshot creates lineage.
    Love lies in that hectic stillness. What suits
    Joans the Surrealist, desire muted
Bursting in the rivers of our dreams—
There black flowers affix their beam.

17.

Once, Ursula, he and I sought beauties
    At the Philadelphia Museum
        & found The Drawings of Joseph Beuys:
    "In Thinking Is Form." Much amused
    By her form, Ted urged her to be his muse
In Paris, as Frida Kahlo's granddaughter.
Ever since, her poems enchant like scripture water.

18.

I smell fresh coffee brewing. My cup's weak.
    These Adirondack chairs seem made
For summer lounging. Kati's likely wreaking
    Havoc on a puzzle. She'll ask for aid,
    But needs next to little. "Author Kincaid.
Seven-letter word beginning with J?" The eager
In-law, I'll chime later "Quai d'Orsay."

HUNTING PARK

1.

I am weary of light over Herring Cove,
    Setting off the urge to pen an aubade.
Yet, all of us in the parking lot drove
    To catch day break the horizon. Cape Cod's
    A place of wit where each their own God.
I've seen her in every glitter. The terns dive
With such passion. My heart breaks. I am alive.

2.

I have a few minutes which to scribble
    More my paranormal memo.
I drink Tedeschi coffee and nibble
    On a muffin. Outside my window,
    Mess of gulls lurk, expecting me to throw
The day's rations. I thumb and eat every crumb.
Thanks to the Fine Arts Work Center, I have come

3.

With Langston to offer my little know-how
    On tinkering poems. This is our father-
Son time. He's on the verge of twelve. How
    Did he grow up so fast? Today, we'll gather
    A gift and visit Stanley Kunitz after
I've talked at length on a poem's rhetorical
Moves, that is, how to make any stanza groove.

4.

I longed for a bar mitzvah when I turned
    His age, some imminent ritual that marked
My neurotic suffering and sudden concern
    For the grave, having realized I'd embarked,
    With no say in the matter, on a slow walk
Towards that unfathomable future
Which seemed aimless as I was sure

5.

How the journey would decisively end.
    (That's no pun.) My start and stop shared
A dot, so I thought. (Well, you're the maven
    Now on this point.) At twelve, I despaired
    Till I read *Le Mythe de Sisyphe*. Camus aired
My darkest thoughts (and the ghetto luckless
Who often pronounced, *I don't give a fuck*).

6.

I wiped the black rings from round my eyes,
    I was the lead singer next for The Cure,
Sans the mop of foppish hair, then devised
    A plan that would give the journey texture,
    Meaning, what Lowell rather reassuringly
Deemed a *loophole for the soul.* I would
Carve these squares, turn speech to shaped wood.

7.

I would make poems that organized time,
    Frame the inevitable so that its trail
Were made visible, a kind of bullet time.
    Notice, in *The Matrix,* each breath exhaled,
    Peerless as the last. Stanley's washed-up whale
Helps sculpt the turning of the years,
Puts us close to mysteries of the spheres.

8.

Art as ritual, said again and again,
    Most recently by DJ Spooky,
Who cites the sound collage as transcendent
    Rite building a nation, our esprit
    De corps. Hip-hop's current genius loci
Believes the cut, scratch, and spin
Amends heteroglossia & situates Bakhtin.

9.

Over the year, I've requested of friends to write
    Postcards to Langston on his birthday,
To share notable moments and rites
    Of passage. We lack non-secular ways
    Of insuring their grasp of that crucial phase:
When they should discover their emotional might,
Thus the custom of visiting a revered poet.

10.

May this letter be kind to time, preserve
    The fibers which bind their inspired intent;
May it revere Ts'ai Lun and his superb
    Dream: pounding wood to pulp, but may it
    Also serve as the "thank you" no amount
Of bread, roses, or honorary degrees
Could ever deign or survive undersiege.

11.

Convention dictates I invoke a god
    Or two. I'll need them; I tend to be long
Winded. For my purposes, a simple nod
    Would do, one that says, "Keep the song
    Taut and chic." and thus my instrument (all wrong
The avant-garde cheeps), the rime royal,
Grounds to some for complete disavowal,

12.

Those who would revoke my poet card,
    Who would charge me with class ascension,
Who would banish me to the stockyard
    Of single-raced anthologies or mention
    Such asinine folly as, "His attention
To rhyme?—weak shot to procure a public.
It's little wonder this will even publish."

13.

To wit, sounds are political; a line reckoned
    Conservative adhering to meter.
While Liberals stream like chanting wiccans,
    Eco-fems enlarge their massive peters.
    The 'Crats compose by space heaters.
Progressives are equally polysemous.
Independents advance on Uncle Remus.

14.

O, Orpheus grant the skills to stir
    The dead like Kanye mixing music with fire,
Spitting souls through wires. Let me chauffeur
    The true and living through muck and mire,
    Rescue the underground so they aim higher.
Grant the gift to chisel words like De Beers.
Let them dangle,—verbal gems for their ears.

ERIE

1.

I put a premium on rhymes—how could I
    Not living the times of the Supa
Emcees where styles are def, lyrics fly,
    Tight the way our minds move over
    Beats and grooves. Our brain matter's
Amped, mic-checked so we non-stop.
My spirit feels echoes thanks to hip-hop.

2.

I thought to send a note to 2Pac,
    Then wondered if he is there with you. Rumor
Has it he's far from dead,—that in fact
    He lives like Assata in Cuba
    Having fled Death Row. His mask consumes us
Still. A rapper shot, a martyr is born.
Sad not the man but an image we mourn:

3.

Party pack tight shots of supersized flesh
    While laughing, sucker-punched to dance,
Each cameo recording resurrects
    Pool-side queries, "How could I just kill a man?"
    An empire croons, toughed-up in a trance.
Imperalism rotates heavy as the world follows
Our nation's mantra: "clothes, bankrolls, and hoes."

4.

Paradise is a checkpoint of virgins
    For which a vest of bombs body-strapped
Blasts shrapnel eyes into martyrdom.
    So they tell us a river of honey maps
    Fluted glasses of desire. On a raft
Float children of Columbine and Palestine,
Bypassing their lives for an ocean of wine.

5.

A cafeteria was all one needed:
    A beat-box firm as the heart. We'd begin
A flow, spitting rhymes that superseded
    Our teacher's verdict: dim-witted children
    Who'll never taste marchand de vin.
Rap's dawning was the earth's reality,
To give a sound to a collective necessity.

6.

Couched in that "We" of the Real always
    Keeping it, that cool defiance, that
Organic e-mail to oppression, hallway
    Leanings and attitudinal grace, that
    Much future you heard, that
Sugar on the Hill ganging up airways,
Those Public Enemy freedom phrases,

7.

Those Boogie Downs and Big Daddy
    Kanes, those Digable Planets & Afro
Names, that Rakim and Mr. Eric B
    Or Disposable Heroes of Hiphoprisy,
    That Salt N Pepa & Roxanne Roxanne,
West coast Coolio and fisted X-Clans,
Those Questing Tribes spitting *Concertos*

8.

Of the Desperadoes, but the Boom Bap's done
    Gone *Jiggy*, and every other word is *Ho*
Or *Niggy*. *Nicca*: still all the same, one
    Frame of the nation that spells hun-
    Ger, like a straw to the brain, video poison
Normalizes the game, our children pointing guns.
We need life like the Fugees need Lauren.

9.

Lest you're worried, we've yet to extinguish
    The human breath; other forms of life
Are game. Our current president's wish?
    To drill Alaska's natural wildlife
    For oil. Thirty-six species of mammal-life,
One hundred types of birds, polar bears,
Made extinct to fuel his earnings per share.

10.

If only we could unravel how to expunge
    Dollars from the democratic process.
Forbes's list sops up elections like sponges.
    Superman no longer beats his chest;
    He merely licks his pen then writes a check.
"Us versus them" is what Nietzsche tallied.
Campaign dinners are hyped pep rallies.

11.

Too much democracy is a leaning tower
    Claim wardens of the two-party regime.
Behind my eyes, sun-lit rain showers,
    A flickering hologram, The Supremes
    Singing "I Hear a Symphony," a stream
Of soft petals drizzling what the country means
To me, an arching tower of rainbow beams.

12.

Where you're at, CNN likely reports:
    Who last booted from empyreal
Heights; what indolent angels fell short
    The good-deeds quota; who's left to heal;
    What new arrivals have seen Ezekiel's
Wheel. I've set the task of bringing up to date
All the news down here; the current state

13.

Of poetry, what's in and what's out, sports,
    Fad diets and more. A prophesy: some
Day we'll dine on info chips in support
    Of ruling elites. Instead of spilling crumbs
    Over *The New York Times*, thumbing
Through say, trade policies, we'll reach consent
By having numbed the discontents—

14.

Instant news granola light beamed via
    Satellite in the mouth: coverage
Of the environment; ProteinPlus for a
    Company man; a square of shredded "yeas"
    For the healthwise, middle-aged
Woman. No youthful rage, no point of view,
No alt. perspective, no making it new.

15.

Tourists have arrived and assumed their place
    On the sands. Each pitched umbrella
Takes us nearer to southern France. The pace
    Of this letter is a little, I know, slow. Fela's
    Playing on the local radio. I'll leaf
These pages with greater speed. I'm off. You've time.
I'll clap our lives as one with a later rhyme.

ALLEGHENY

1.

What privilege I flaunt discarding time
    Like a swatch of faded, blue-jean sky
Addressing you as though the poem a clothesline
    & we, two cups that connect, speaking high
    Above the city—or is it more like I
Slow earth's spinning with my finger?
My pen a needle where the song lingers.

2.

Not out for the epic, I want a vault
    For my verbal wealth. I want a form
For my lyrical stealth. I want a malt
    To toast the public's health. I want a storm
    On my perfect shelf. I mourned
Your loss on the phone with Marie Howe.
You were her first love. I said, "How

3.

Would she want us to remember her?"
    She said, "As we do—in verse."
Then, "Do you think she'll reply to a letter?"
    She said, "The dead are terse."
    I got it, then I said, "Hearses
Should speed to graves in processions.
The living outnumber their phantoms."

4.

"Lady Paul Laurence Dunbar" is how
    I would have dispatched in your youth,—
Mother Keziah, assured you'd plough
    Words for dialectical truths,
    Named you thus. An insatiable sweet tooth
You had early for concentrated rhymes,
Flavorful as raspberry, orange, or lime.

5.

Possibly I want a hero, too. Tis
    Dry, true—those documentaries come
February striving for racial bliss.
    I would rather have sung "We Shall Overcome"
    At a Super Bowl than one more mind-numb
-Ing black-and-white clip of the unnamed hosed
In prayer. I would rather whole episodes

6.

Featuring year-round *Biography*'s:
    Black poets, surgeons, priests.
How more acrobatic do our teeth need to be?
    How many more laughs can a feast
    Of eyes, hard boiled, bulging, the leitmotif
Of the downtrodden graphic terror,
Sustain the birth of a nation? The nearer

7.

The prize, when some standup out-bugs
    His eyes. Law-upholding laughter
Follows like a stutter step as the Strug
    -Gle giggles, and a world of sufferers
    Side-splits away their tears. That's why *Nigger*
No longer sticks like cotton in the throat.
Some black comics are the worst turncoats.

8.

Many dance to forget. I knew a giant
    Who rolled down Broad blasting Led
Zeppelin in a ride. His gentle spirit
    Streamed along till his pain cracked & bled
    & left two brackish hawsers. He shed
What ached by shuttling open-aired, a means
I'd likely never forget, the scream

9.

Of art, blood music caught in the strum
    Uncoiling from bedsprings. It's there
At our begetting, hurt that becomes
    A singular song. We add to the blare
    & din. We give it a window by a chair
& listen, nodding heads, rubbing chins,
& throw our hands up as if greeting friends.

10.

I, myself, emerged from a dark cave lured
    By history and two visions. A romantic,
I stood in my b-boy stance, arms ruled,
    Angled back, head posed for the authentic—
    Up joined the Dark Room Collective.
Were I in Kentucky I would, even then,
Have united with the Affrilachians,

11.

So strong the urge to place my pen aside
    My generation. Ellis was our Pound.
We, the inheritors of your black pride,
    & he, loudest inkslinger with Strange, found
    A cadre to unselfconsciously sound
Off Hayden, Baraka, Dove, and Wright,
To become our next black literary lights.

12.

Light does not exist in a coffin,
*   Both merely signifiers asserts Derrida.*
I'm off for a cup of Starbucks coffee,
*   & a lifespan sipped on DVD.*
*   Avoid the headlines by the jelly*
Beans. How queasy war next to tins of mints.
Have you bought Musicology *by Prince?*

13.

Who did we not celebrate? America could
    Never deal with a diverse canon of poets.
I mean what it really means, and not just a cold
    Few hiding out in "Separate but equal"
    Magazines, really face a people's poetry.
This was the aim of the DRC,
To test the puddles of white supremacy.

NORTH PHILADELPHIA

1.

Baltimore Harbor is foggy this morn
   Like my head, another AWP
Conference, too many cocktails adorned
   In a hotel bar, too many thorny
   Conversations. Many wear their scorn
On their sleeves and talk of chopping folks
At the knees. Others yield to dirty jokes.

2.

My neck hurts. I've said a hundred hellos.
   I've gone down elevators and faced
My ghoulish past. At times I wanted to know
   & sought a name tag. My overnight case
   Hasn't arrived. I thought I'd touch base
To relieve some of the low-stakes tension,
Time to transport to the fourth dimension.

3.

Before I do, just a word about this scene.
    Careerism runs rampant, less so vision.
Today's poem is like a pair of Levi's jeans.
    It seeks to create its own tradition,
    So, many wear limited edition
Black dungarees. Blameless, I'd wish
They'd consider taking less fashionable risks.

4.

Any scribble these days passes for poem.
    Overly Inventive holds sway.
Mr. Too Earnest yearns. Mrs. Forms
    Wants in, but imagines her stays
    Against mayhem causes malaise.
Standards float untethered to any school.
We've thrown out the farm with the rules.

5.

The wars have toned down, a truce struck
    Between the camps. No one's holding hands
Or hurling stones, unless you're a critic.
    God forbid, a free-thinking woman:
    Helen V. sizzles in the frying pan;
Poor Alice Q. takes it on the chin;
Rita voodooed to a doll of pushpins.

6.

This feels a little too insiderish,
    A little too gossipy, a little
Too off the beaten. Best to pass up
    The bright bulb of tittle-tattle
    Where whispers pool and settle,
All this week, heads turn, then ignite
To a heap of moths zapped at night.

7.

The strange terrain ourselves we tour
    In Art. You said it first: art hurts,
The reflection fogless by the hour,
    Oblivion girdles the frame, distorts,
    Makes plain, we are not who we say we are.
In the showdown between Art & Life,
Jump cut & *Face/Off*, the *Hard-Boiled* fight.

8.

Tonight, I'll crumple like a thundercloud
    & tent my head in a trench coat.
A litany of leaves mists my eyes, enshrouds
    The orchestral rage of grace notes..
    Think of all the veins of a straining throat.
Think of Amiri squatting on time's hoard.
Think of the beast impaled on his sword.

9.

This flat beach of a page speaks
  Beyond the grave, a summoning akin
To Lazarus of Bethany who leaped
  From his sepulcher, as from a bunk
  Bed, & sparked with Dante that noble trend:
The dead holding hands. In dark woods,
The living go on separated by blood,

10.

Yet join in fear, which is to say, we are
  Never alone. I throw up a prop
Of firs with their tremble of supple tops and smear
  The scene a blackish green and propel
  Us to Rousseau's *Carnival*,
Then dot the sky a silken moon,
Then a soft stroke for a road, pluming

11.

The canvas like a blade of petrified
  Smoke. In this mise-en-scène, the soul's
Less an abstraction, less terrorized
  Like Little Red Riding finding solace
  In the offering, a basket of sweet rolls,
Sliced apples, victuals for the wolf's
Hanker. What-if said disciples followed

12.

The loathsome heed, "Never talk to strangers"?
    Turning away, we write and often plunge
To routine deaths, and give over to the inner ogre
    Who directs and solos our grungy
    Ecstasy of transport, a potential trudge
Of desultory dimensions. My Virgil,
You'd have polished off this couplet with virgule.

13.

I'll say it,—poetry debates are quite
    The bore, many rowed in bad taste (like the one
Page vs. Stage), more so when bombs make bites
    Of all we write. Performance poets run
    The risk of outperforming the poem. Some
Gesture little or too much. Many should quit,
Just drop the mic. Others rely on wit

14.

Too heavily in the region of sex,
    Hoping to score the hottie up front, or
Mutter strings of words at best didactic.
    I put them on mute, weak masturbators
    Of verbal wicks who believe they're clever
And intelligent, who squint in the glare
Of stagelights, looking for their audience.

15.

What happened in youth? What makes them seek
    Such glory? They should be off campaigning,
Telling their story. Less than unique,
    They'd make great guests of Oprah's confessing
    What abuse they beat to acting success.
Maybe, it's right, they name their work pieces.
There's no other word to rhyme but feces.

16.

Too quick to dismiss so-called academic
    Poets as earless elitists out of touch,
They reveal how massive their ignorance
    For many slipped in with luck,
    And not respected all that much
By colleagues who view them intelopers
Lacking rigor, or worse, alcoholic bipolars.

17.

Truth be told, I dabbled in performance
    Poetry. I was not myself on stage
Mouthing my dithyrambs. Backed by a band,
    I tried a little humor, then lots of rage,
    Then a syncopated flow to assuage
Those expecting a more hip-notic stream,
Fluid like the art of Carrie Mae Weems.

18.

Speaking of academics and their lot,
    A few approach. Concurrent sessions
With titles like *The Road to the Bon Mot*
    Or *The Future of the Sestina*
    Alas, reflects of our profession
Its sorry state. Yet, we are moved to attend
By the MFA and its invisible hand.

SUSQUEHANNA-DAUPHIN

1.

I've arisen to dawn at The Frost Place.
    I've jerry-rigged a desk by the window
Overlooking a trail. I'm the new face
    Of mountain poetry. Tourists come and go
    Off hours though, interrupting my ego's
Pursuit, a lasting chamber for my soul.
The worst is when I munch a bowl

2.

Of Frosted Flakes, pacing in my briefs
    And a right curious family peers in.
They visor their foreheads; disbelief
    Creeps across their face. I am the old man's
    Ghost as were twenty-six beforehand.
Summers we come to haunt the porch,
As Billy Matthews put it, "to scorch

3.

Off / morning fog," which I poke with my pen
    And swirl. It gathers cobwebby-like round
A thought I curl then write to its end.
    The broccoli-topped trees I see down
    Straight after that to Route 93. Tourists abound
This time of year. I wish I could install
On deck *(I've not the word for what they're called)*

4.

One of those standing boardwalk binoculars,
    Requiring a quarter that opens a shutter,
Then, suddenly the ocean's particulars
    Are as intimate as your face; buttery,
    Midday light they'd see, my mind sputtering
To complete these stanzas stacked like bricks,
Or mornings when I am my own exhibitionist,

5.

Catching me in the mirror dancing nude,
    Or toweling my hands, or stirring brown sugar
In my tea, in any case my back rudely
    To their probing eyes wide as arugula.
    To protect my Chi, I'd hang a sign: *Beggars
Disallowed* or *Peace God* or *Shhhhh! Poet at Work.*
To really back them off: *Beware of Jerk.*

6.

Yesterday, I met Superman's dad, come
    To talk about Frost in Russia. Nikita
Apparently liked the old man's homespun
    Demeanor, but regarded Akhmatova
    With greater suspicion. Marina
Tsvetaeva was Brodsky's fave of the four
Pillars of Soviet verse, Boris

7.

Pasternak and Osip Mandlestam
    Being the other two. (A thought: I miss
The Red Square, that lounge bar I stammered
    Home nights raving my life mission:
    Black Marxist down with liberating the pissed
Off, poverty-stricken of North Philly.
But, how to agitate a nation fed doses of Jerry

8.

Springer?) I name Brodsky in my top five.
    He'd surely have this poem clinched by now.
I'd send him a carbon copy were he alive,
    Wrapped in rice paper, tied with a bow.
    I imagine he'd bend over, let out a howl.
Maybe, you can let him read a bit of this.
On second thought, let's keep down our risks.

9.

I drove here Fourth of July to grant my gift
    Of time a symbolic cast. I inherit
A fit distrust of patriotic rites, miffed
    And aware of the "unholy license"
    That is, as Frederick Douglass phrased it,
The country's "boasted liberty." Fireworks
Mark our jubilee; one more year to shirk

10.

The crucial act of accountability:
    Reparations. Some ideas: change Martin
Luther King Day to 3rd of July;
    Mail free poems by black citizens,
    Offer counseling to those of African
Descent. Who do I kid? In my time,
Likely never will the heinous crime

11.

Of American slavery be put to rest.
    We are joined as if in marital gloom;
The scar we inherit is a wedding chest
    Of lynchings and hatreds exhumed
    Each generation. Forever doomed,
Each wishing for the sword that severs all,
We return to stage for our curtain calls.

12.

Last week, a bat flew in. I thought it was
    The old man come to reclaim his hearth.
You saw *lightning in his eyes*. I saw
    Fear beading in the dark. His verse haunts
    American Lit. classes and for now stunts
My pen. That's all the better. The time crunch
Gives pause. My belly growls. I'm off to lunch.

CECIL B. MOORE

1.

Gwen, I am glad you're not living at this hour,
    For we are like the kid pushed in a yard
Who pushes back, then finding his power,
    Becomes the bully with no regard
    For what hates he sows. How soon our scars
Fade. The light of an empire ages. Daily seas
Rumble below repeating man's history.

2.

September triggered a rash
    Of abuses, all around. I am concerned
For Langston's future. We are not rich
    Enough to avoid conscription. He'll earn,
    His stripes, I hope, by not harming
Other parents' children, but performing acts
Of diplomacy, which today smack

3.

Of the dress rehearsal before the attack.
   How would you have responded? Images
Of men and women beheaded or stacked
   Before a camera, the mental war waged
   In our name? Who foretold the carnage?
Or the beast beneath our skin? how we proclaim
Civility, then digitize the cave whence we came?

4.

Our psyche takes the beating, six hooded
   Iraqis lurk behind us in our dreams.
When the axe swings, we awaken, doomed
   To not hear the Sanskrit above our screams.
   My grandfather came on the scene the same
Year as you. Stunning to think of the horrors
Of the century in his head. In a corner,

5.

The child in him crouches as the room darkens.
   He was born to a world at war & expects
To die a night of bombs evening the score. When
   I fire-up my laptop & cam, he shirks
   & cannot take more of the world at work,
Enough electric spanking he seems to say,
Nor believes men on the moon, to this day.

6.

Question: How much headway can we take?
    Are we advancing faster than our blood
Courses? Much we've already taken
    At a lightning pace, over-flooding
    Perhaps what our brains can endure. You'd
Giggle at the breakthroughs of the past decade,
For one, robots disarming bombs in caves.

7.

The wireless world we live permits instant
    Admission. The Internet shrinks the globe.
We've hotspots to our bank accounts,
    The Hague, stores, our homes. I can disrobe
    On a beach and never cease the work mode,
Like registering students for my classes,
Or answering e-mails from the lads & lasses.

8.

We've developed at last alternative
    Ways to move our cars. Hybrid engines
Free us all the more from excessive
    Costs at the pump. In our fin
    De siècle despair of OPEC's siphoning
Of American pockets, I predict, once
We're through all together with oil, the only

9.

Vehicles left to fuel will be machines
    Of war, our children sure to become Lowell's
Ghosts orbiting forever on a big screen,
    A reality show we will likely sell
    To the public as a means of swelling
National pride,—in our time, a hollow value,
The gist zapped from the red, white, and blue.

10.

Of TVs, we hunger for bigger screens, better
    Sounds. XM & Sirius broaden
The waves with satellites and crystal-clear
    Tunes or the news. The man in Tienanmen
    Square and I can synchronize more than
Our thirst for democracy. We can get our fill
On Dylan, Coldplay, and Cypress Hill.

11.

Kids no longer devour dots. Gaming videos
    Turn them to fighters who hunt bad guys.
Fully armed imaginary worlds like Halo
    Insure no one different catches the prize.
    In Grand Theft Auto, they've even devised
Squalid streets that let you explore the thug
Within: soccer moms jacking rides for drugs.

12.

Computer chips are smaller than fingerprints.
    We've acronyms for it all: with GPS
You never guess where you're going. With Sprint
    Phones just about anyone can be a spy.
    Every cell is a cam, and every cam an eye.
Picture the universe through a single bubble,
Planets billions of years away through the Hubble.

13.

An unmanned spacecraft landed on Mars.
    iPods will never leave you without a song.
My students walk the quad like Martians.
    Biotech firms go cloning along.
    Stem cells can remake our bones strong.
We are mapping the human genome;
We'll soon design kids to match our homes.

14.

I looked you up this morning. Eighty-one
    Thousand results with audio links,
Biographies, profiles, and pics, your life summed
    & presented to the tyro in a blink.
    Substitute the Cartesian logic, I think
To "I Google, therefore I am," and you've
Uncovered our zeitgeist, the groove

15.

Of an era, our mark on earth measured
    In binary codes, not by deeds, which total
Many for you. So many claim your sway, treasure
    Your artful phrasings and praise, fell under
    Your spell like electricity to thunder.
I, like them, value you above all else,
Indispensable poet of the public's health.

16.

I begin this stop all wrong: you *should be*
    Living at this hour. We need your bolts
& resounding poems like we need Sweet Honey
    In the Rock's sacred songs, a revolt
    Against plain figurings, new and bold
Metaphors to help us keep people always
In vision, to fight the corporate bug away.

GIRARD

1.

Canopies of red oak trees line the campus
    At James Madison University, site
Again of the most esteemed conference since
    The poetry gatherings at Fisk in the sixties.
    I've found an overhang of branches before tonight's
Awards presentation to sit and pen this note.
First, a swig of tea. Now, let me clear my throat.

2.

Ten years since last Furious Flower,
    We gather in the '04. Dr. Gabbin has once
More arranged a bouquet (to replay our
    Garden motif again) to pronounce
    Our blossoming and wicked grace.
You are here in spirit, your name evoked
On many occasions. You know black folk

3.

With all their conjuring, some carelessly
    Calling forth haints. (Let's pause to enjoy
How haint echoes haunt. The journey
    Between the *i* and *u* is topoi
    For etymologists or smitten love boys,
Or have we lost taste for such pleasures
As the hidden jewel of linguistic treasures?)

4.

Where was I? That's right, JMU. Virginia.
    The flowers prove more luminous
If we pick those poets on the margins
    For our floral arrangment though not as
    Loud or political or choose to stress less
Their mold: from Mackey to Mullens,
Afaa to Wright, I'd throw a party

5.

For those literary lights; Wilkinson
    For his Southern flair and Giscombe's
Cerebral ear; Erica Hunt and Kocher
    For their unsigned hype; combless
    Shepherd for his post-lyric play; I'm at home
Reading Crystal or Shara in May. Many
Are conspicuously absent to my dismay.

6.

What's lacking is a comprehensive discourse
    On poetics that's not race-bound. Resist-
ance is a given, par for the course,
    Like Gamble, Huff, and the Philly Sound. Permit
    More utterances that reveal the size of it,
The range of black humanity, and the conference
Shows up transparent, merely a kind of fence.

7.

Somehow, art must transcend "I'm blacker
    Than you," a mask that corresponds by degrees
To what we've culled and conceived of blackness,
    A kind of palimpsest on the skin. To seize
    The nature of the self like a warm breeze
Coming off the sea, herein lies the power
Of that garden and its prurient flowers.

8.

O, to possess the vision of Sebastiao
    Salgado, that talismanic gift, to frame
The infinitely suffering thing, to plough
    Our common plight and slyly take aim.
    Your preference for "Black" as the name
Uniting all Africans né brown people
Winningly made my art, like his, global.

9.

We move in tow from concurrent panels
    On the state of black verse. Cruse's
Crisis of the Negro Intellectual
    Crosses my mind, the static bruises
    We tend, the anchored questions we renew
As if scripted, déjà vu's double click,
Or the chink in the grid of The Matrix.

10.

What we profess: black poetry
    As the eloquent testament and record,
A tacit argument for a greater liberty
    In America. Readers are rewarded,
    Embodying an interiority
They need to possess their lyric freedom,
Their moral lineage, and borrowed drums.

11.

We make life possible for each other, said
    Martin Buber, if only for a moment.
"All real living is meeting." Breaking bread,
    I propose, calls us to the presentness
    Of others seated, too. So, we consent
To the same encounter reading lyrics,
More of the journey between I and You.

12.

The conference readings this go-round lack
    For want of you. Ms. Lucille aroused
An ovation. She seems poised to beat back
    Time and inherit your purse. Campus boughs
    Above me nod as if to agree. I browse
The sky and seek exemplary moments that linger:
Haki name-calling Gates was a stinger.

13.

That, I naively wish would go away,
    The legacy, too, of the Black Arts,
Talking about folks as if to slay
    Their reputation, as if to tear apart
    The spines of their books. René Descartes:
Omnia apud me poetica fiunt. Oops!
I misquote by design. Call in the troops.

14.

Possibly, this is what you heard at Fisk,
    The damaging rhetoric targeting
The so-called *Negroes*. A Pulitzer can put you at
    Odds with your skin. Upon hearing
    Amiri and how accommodationist leanings
Are mild forms of *shuck*, it must have struck
That you'd become on stage a lame duck.

FAIRMONT

1.

Ten years ago, the night of the awards
    Banquet, the younger set showed up,
Our Red Roof room to examine the sword
    We'd just been given and to sip from the cup.
    Okay, this wasn't Excalibur, but
More, we gathered to share our poems, the open
Mic had yet to storm campus programs.

2.

Kevin opened with a poem by Hayden,
    Prefaced the recitation with a reminder.
How Fisk's unrewarded poet, an Auden
    Acolyte, went through the grinder
    Of black scrutiny by some of the honored
There that night. Two of the older, less talented
Followed, chiding us for having misspent

3.

Our college tuition; the misinformation
    Was rampant and wide of the mark,
Which began a row, a quarrelsome
    Spat between the generations. That spark
    Lit the Shenandoah National Park
With knockdown, verbal blows that purged
Us from the thumb of the Black Arts.

4.

I can share more insight as to why
    My encomium, a word I choose
Over panegyric, which to my eyes
    Looks like a Greek bottle of booze.
    One could tag the strains that serve the muse,
Including what Stephen Henderson proffers:
Black speech and music at the poetry altar.

5.

Yet, we cannot overlook how we inspire
    Each other into song, thus I propose
The praise poem as one of our chief desires,
    A form that allows us to compose
    Heroic additives such as Oscar Micheaux
To what's lacking in the textbooks,
Historical figures that go overlooked.

6.

Just think of all the poems to Malcolm
    Little or John Coltrane. Fast-forward
To Regie Gibson, transformed to become
    The verbal strum of Hendrix's guitar,
    Breathing back his fire chords.
Then, return to Hayden's "Frederick Douglass,"
Ideal sonnet to cover in any class.

7.

All that to say, I write in the tradition.
    Giving you your props and positions.
Less a search-and-rescue mission,
    (Will someone testify to Owen Dodson?
    Here in the Russell Atkins or Helene Johnson?)
More, writing you is like my literary mission
To extend your life's work and distinction.

8.

I would propose your corpus as one big
    Encomium. What young critic would take on
Supporting such an assertion? If the blues is our dig
    At the existential press, the praise poem's
    Our loudest handclap to survival. *Da jawn*
As we say around the way. Shout out to Okayplayer
And Philly homegirl, Bahamadia.

9.

What do we have here? A cypher has broken
    Out. Where's my camera? A circle of words,
Freestyling returned, ancient as this autumn,
    Reddish air. I have the silly urge
    To break in, a little flow of my own, stir
The unbroken spirit that has us return
To ancestral waters. Here's my next sojourn.

SPRING GARDEN

1.

When you have forgotten (to bring into
   Play that fragrant morsel of rhetoric,
Crisp as autumnal air), when you
   Have forgotten, say, sun-lit corners, brick
   Full of skyline, rowhomes, smokestacks,
Billboards, littered rooftops & wondered
What bread wrappers reflect of our hunger,

2.

When you have forgotten wide-brimmed hats,
   Sunday back-seat leather rides & church,
The doorlock like a silver cane, the broad backs
   Swaying or the great moan deep churning,
   & the shimmer flick of flat sticks, the lurch
Forward, skip, hands up Ailey-esque drop,
When you have forgotten the meaningful bop,

3.

Hustlers and their care-what-may, blasé
   Ballet and flight, when you have forgotten
Scruffy yards, miniature escapes, the way
   Laundry lines strung up sag like shortened
   Smiles, when you have forgotten the Fish Man
Barking his catch in inches up the street
"I've got porgies. I've got trout. Feeesh

4.

Man," or his scoop and chain scale,
   His belief in shad and amberjack; when
You have forgotten Ajax and tin pails,
   Blue crystals frothing on marble front
   Steps Saturday mornings, or the garden
Of old men playing checkers, the curbs
White-washed like two lines out to the burbs,

5.

Or the hopscotch squares painted new
   In the street, the pitter-patter of feet
Landing on rhymes. "How do you
   Like the weather, girls? All in together girls,
   January, February, March, April . . ."
The jump ropes' portentous looming,
Their great, aching love blooming.

124

6.

When you have forgotten packs of grape
    Flavored Now & Laters, the squares
Of sugar flattening on the tongue, the elation
    You felt reaching into the corner-store jar,
    Grasping a handful of Blow Pops, candy bars
With names you didn't recognize but came
To learn. All the turf battles. All the war games.

7.

When you have forgotten popsicle stick
    Races along the curb and hydrant fights,
Then, retrieve this letter from your stack
    I've sent by clairvoyant post & read by light.
    For it brought me as much longing and delight.
This week's Father's Day; I've a long ride to Philly.
I'll give this to Gramps, then head to Black Lily.